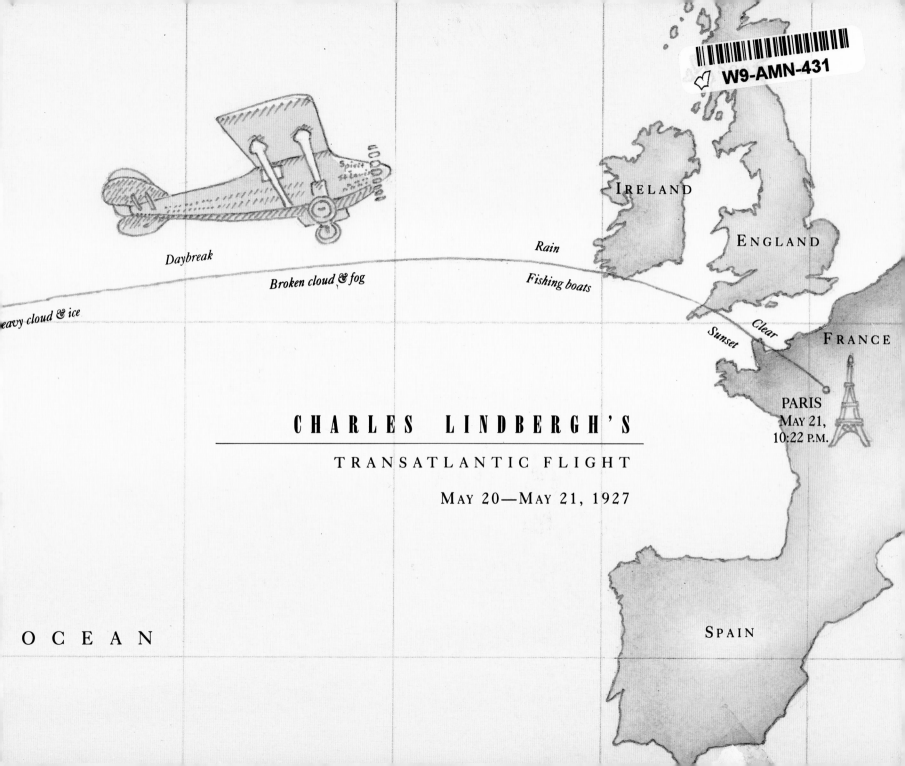

W9-AMN-431

IRELAND

ENGLAND

FRANCE

Rain

Daybreak

Broken cloud & fog

Fishing boats

Clear

Sunset

Heavy cloud & ice

PARIS
MAY 21,
10:22 P.M.

CHARLES LINDBERGH'S

TRANSATLANTIC FLIGHT

MAY 20—MAY 21, 1927

SPAIN

OCEAN

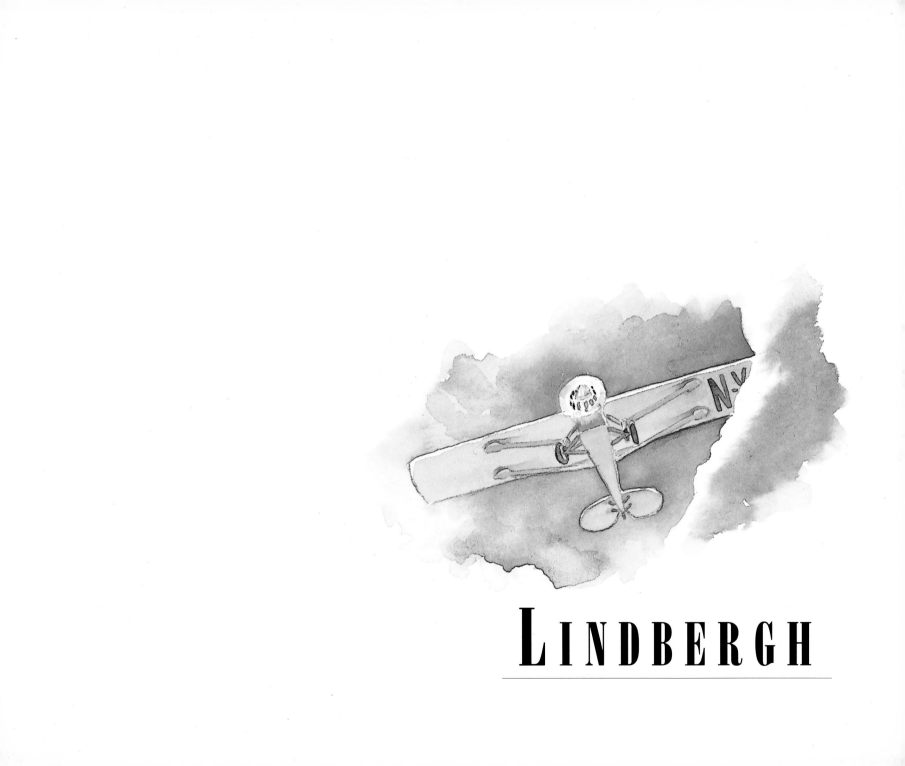

LINDBERGH

LINDBERGH

CHRIS L. DEMAREST

CROWN PUBLISHERS, INC.   *New York*

3.1489-00-3.1 9720

B71 $15.00

When Charles Lindbergh was born, not a single plane flew in the American sky. The year was 1902. Automobiles were rare, and postage was only two cents.

Charles grew up on a small farm in Little Falls, Minnesota, a lumber town on the Mississippi River. His family called the place Camp. There was no electricity, no telephone, and food was delivered from town once a week. Sometimes Charles went to town for supplies. He borrowed his father's bicycle, but because it was so big he had to stand up and pedal with one leg under the crossbar.

Charles was always busy. He built a boat, a pair of stilts, a concrete duck pond, and a tree house complete with a trapdoor for his father's feet to hang out.

Food was kept in an icebox. It was Charles's job to keep it filled with ice blocks. Because the blocks were so heavy, he used a cart, planks of wood, and pulleys to make the job of moving them from the icehouse to the kitchen easier.

One day Charles's father came home with a Model T Ford. Charles was overjoyed. He loved standing on the running board of the car while his father drove. Later, Charles would learn to drive the car, and he became a much better driver than either of his parents. By age eleven he would be doing most of the family driving.

One day while Charles was playing in the attic, he heard an unusual noise. Racing to the window, he spotted a biplane loping up the river, barely above the treetops. He was eight years old. From that moment Charles dreamed of almost nothing but flying.

Charles grew to love speed. When he was eighteen, he bought an Excelsior motorcycle. Two months later, he left the farm for college in Wisconsin.

He had always loved to tinker and had become an excellent mechanic, so at college Charles chose to study engineering. But he still dreamed of flying, and school proved to be too dull for him. After two years he dropped out. Astride his motorcycle, he headed for Lincoln, Nebraska, and flying school. Unfortunately, the school closed before Charles received his pilot's license.

Lindbergh persuaded a barnstorming pilot to take him along as his mechanic. Barnstorming was a name for flying from town to town taking people for airplane rides. To attract crowds, Lindbergh would "wing-walk" as they flew low over the towns they visited. He quickly became known as Daredevil Lindbergh. Always with the barnstormers was their mascot—a fox terrier named Booster.

Having learned to fly, Lindbergh traded in his motorcycle for a war-surplus airplane known as a "Jenny." He barnstormed on his own but wanted to become a better pilot. In 1924 he joined the U.S. Army Air Service Reserve to learn to fly the latest aircraft.

The following year, airmail service in the United States was extended to the Midwest. Excited by the prospect of a job that would allow him to fly all the time, Lindbergh joined the service. He flew the route between St. Louis and Chicago. It was a hazardous job, involving flying in all kinds of weather. Twice he was forced to parachute to safety.

As dangerous as it was, Lindbergh grew bored. One night, on a routine run, he recalled reading of a prize for the first person to fly nonstop across the Atlantic Ocean between New York and Paris. For seven years people had tried but failed. Almost immediately Lindbergh began making plans.

Lindbergh had some money saved, but not enough to build the kind of plane that could make the transatlantic flight. He persuaded a group of St. Louis businessmen to back him and hired a small company in San Diego, California, called Ryan Airlines to build his plane. He named it *The Spirit of St. Louis.*

Others had tried—and failed—to make the crossing in planes with two or more engines. To save weight, Lindbergh chose to fly alone in a single-engine plane.

Because so much fuel would be needed to make the long flight, the area between the engine and the pilot's seat became the fuel tank. This meant Lindbergh would have no forward vision. So a periscope was added to the left window.

Lindbergh knew that others were planning attempts to win the prize, so work on *The Spirit of St. Louis* was completed in record time. In only sixty days the plane was ready. Lindbergh flew from California to New York, where he would begin his adventure.

Lindbergh's anxiety about being beaten grew as his takeoff for Paris was delayed by bad weather in New York. But after eight long days the weather finally cleared. On May 20, 1927, at 7:52 A.M. after barely two hours of sleep, Charles Lindbergh gave the signal that he was ready. Slowly the plane gathered speed as it rolled across the wet, muddy runway of Roosevelt Field. Loaded down with 450 pounds of fuel, *The Spirit of St. Louis* cleared the telephone lines at the end of the runway by only twenty feet. Then it disappeared into the morning mist.

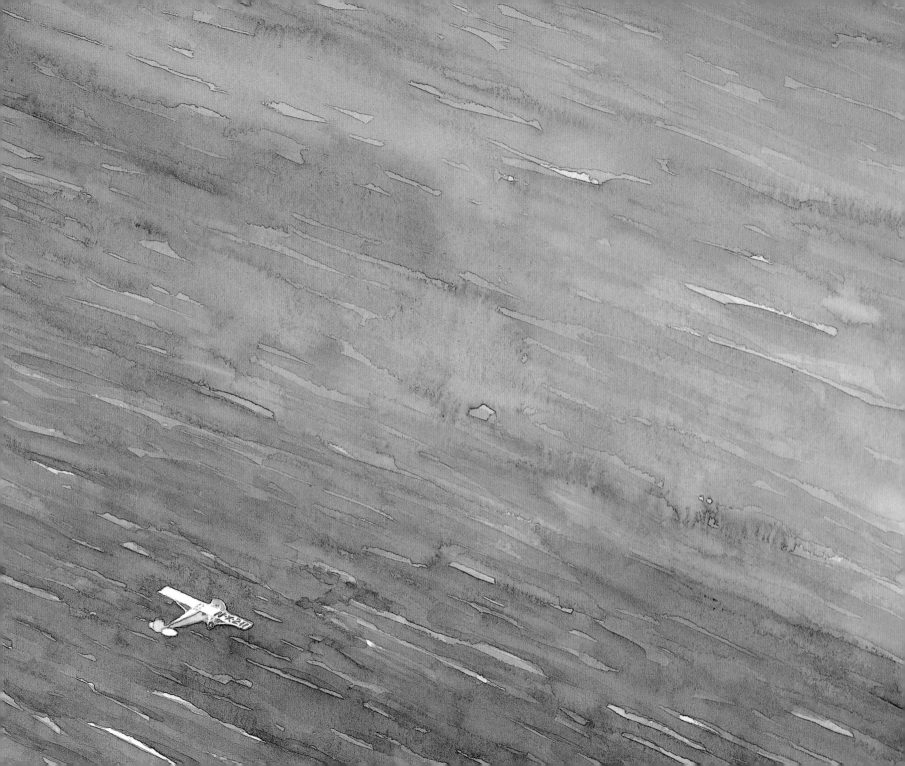

Shortly after takeoff, the plane emerged into brilliant sunshine.
Lindbergh flew the length of Long Island, passed over Cape Cod,
Massachusetts, and angled toward Nova Scotia, Canada, hugging
the coast.

Eleven hours into the flight he reached Newfoundland.
From there on it would be only open ocean all the way to Europe.
With the sun setting, *The Spirit of St. Louis* flew on into the night.

Cruising through towering storm clouds, Lindbergh was horrified to find ice forming on the wings. Too much ice could cause the plane to lose altitude and crash. Fortunately, the moment the plane emerged from the clouds, the ice began falling off. By weaving around the clouds, the problem was solved. But as moonlight flooded the tiny cockpit, the biggest problem remained: how to stay awake.

Daylight brought no relief. At times the flight was dreamlike as Lindbergh would wake with a start, realizing the plane was wandering.

Speeding along just above the waves, sticking his head out the window, hoping the cold wind would keep him awake, Lindbergh spotted a small fishing fleet through the mist. He circled one boat and called out, "Which way to Ireland?" There was no answer except a surprised stare from a fisherman.

The second sunset of the flight found
Lindbergh across the English Channel above
Cherbourg, France. Following the River Seine
toward Paris, Lindbergh knew he was just
hours away from completing his journey. He
took the first bite of a sandwich he had bought
in a delicatessen before leaving New York.

At 10:22 P.M. on May 21, more than thirty-three hours after leaving
New York, *The Spirit of St. Louis* touched down at Le Bourget airfield near
Paris. Crowds poured onto the field cheering and calling Lindbergh's
name. News of his triumph quickly spread back to New York and around
the globe. This quiet young man from a rural town in Minnesota was
suddenly a hero to the world. His life would never be the same.

AFTERWORD

Lindbergh's careful planning had paid off, and when he landed in Paris there was enough fuel left in *The Spirit of St. Louis*'s tank to have carried him as far as Italy. The flight earned him the $25,000 Orteig Prize for the first person to fly nonstop from New York to Paris.

On his return to the United States, Lindbergh was greeted by tickertape parades in dozens of cities. Almost immediately he began a 40,000-mile world goodwill tour in *The Spirit of St. Louis*. His final flight in that plane was to Washington, D.C.; he delivered it to the Smithsonian Institution on April 30, 1928. It remains on display there at the Air and Space Museum.

While visiting Mexico during the tour, Lindbergh met Anne Morrow, daughter of Dwight Morrow, the U.S. ambassador. Anne shared Charles's enthusiasm for adventure and, after their marriage in May 1929, flew with him as navigator and radio operator. Together they charted new air routes to Europe (flying as far north as Greenland), Asia, Africa, and South America. Once, upon seeing their plane the *Sirius*, a young Eskimo boy called it *Tingmissartoq*, meaning "the one who flies like a big bird." The *Sirius* is also in the Air and Space Museum.

Charles and Anne found time to write several books. *The Spirit of St. Louis* won Charles Lindbergh the Pulitzer Prize. Anne's book, *The Gift from the Sea*, is still widely read today. During their travels they began noticing how badly people were treating the planet. They became lifelong conservationists, working to save many endangered species.

Lindbergh remained interested in aviation throughout his life. He advised private companies as well as the U.S. government on the development of air routes, rocketry, space exploration, and aviation in general. And though he had never been much of a student, his love of science and nature led him to help develop the first heart pump successfully used to keep patients alive during transplant operations.

Charles Lindbergh died on August 26, 1974, at his favorite home, in Hawaii, surrounded by the animals he loved so much.

Charles Lindbergh and Anne Morrow Lindbergh in Japan, 1931.

Charles Lindbergh age nine with his dog, Dingo.

Lindbergh and *The Spirit of St. Louis* in early May 1927, before the transatlantic flight. The letters "NYP" on the tail stand for "New York–Paris."

RESOURCE GUIDE

BOOKS

Roxanne Chadwick, *Anne Morrow Lindbergh: Pilot and Poet* (Lerner Publications Company, 1987).

Ted Gilman, *The Flight* (Heather Ridge Publications, 1986).

Charles A. Lindbergh, *Boyhood on the Mississippi: A Reminiscent Letter* (Minnesota Historical Society, 1972).

Charles A. Lindbergh, *The Spirit of St. Louis* (Charles Scribners Sons, 1953).

Francis Trevelyan Miller, *Lindbergh: His Story in Pictures* (Northstar-Maschek Books, 1989).

FILMS

Lindbergh. A PBS film in the "American Experience" series (PBS Video).

The Spirit of St. Louis. With James Stewart as Charles Lindbergh (Warner Brothers Video).

PLACES TO VISIT

Lindbergh Historical Site, Route 3, Box 245, Lindbergh Drive, Little Falls, Minnesota 56345.

Jefferson Memorial Museum/Missouri Historical Society, Forest Park, Lindell Boulevard & DeBaliviere, St. Louis, Missouri 63112.

Smithsonian Institution Air and Space Museum, Washington, D.C. 20560.

To Robert Demarest (1921-1989), a pilot

Special thanks to:
The people at the Lindbergh Historical Site; Andrea Cascardi; Simon Boughton;
Bud Allison at the Air and Space Museum; A. L.; and Laura Gillespie

Copyright © 1993 by Chris L. Demarest
All rights reserved. No part of this book may be reproduced or transmitted in any form or by any
means, electronic or mechanical, including photocopying, recording, or by any information storage
and retrieval system, without permission in writing from the publisher. Published by Crown
Publishers, Inc., a Random House company, 201 East 50th Street, New York, New York 10022.
CROWN is a trademark of Crown Publishers, Inc.
Manufactured in the United States of America

Library of Congress Cataloging-in-Publication Data
Demarest, Chris L.
Lindbergh / by Chris L. Demarest.
p. cm.
Summary: Describes the early life of Charles Lindbergh, leading up to his
history-making transatlantic flight in 1927.
1. Lindbergh, Charles A. (Charles Augustus), 1902-1974—Juvenile literature.
2. Air pilots—United States—Biography—Juvenile literature.
[1. Lindbergh, Charles A. (Charles Augustus), 1902-1974. 2. Air pilots.] I. Title.
TL540.L5D475   1993
                      629.13'092—dc20
[B]   92-41845

ISBN0-517- 58718-1 (trade)
0-517-58719-X (lib. bdg.)

1 2 3 4 5 6 7 8 9 10
First Edition

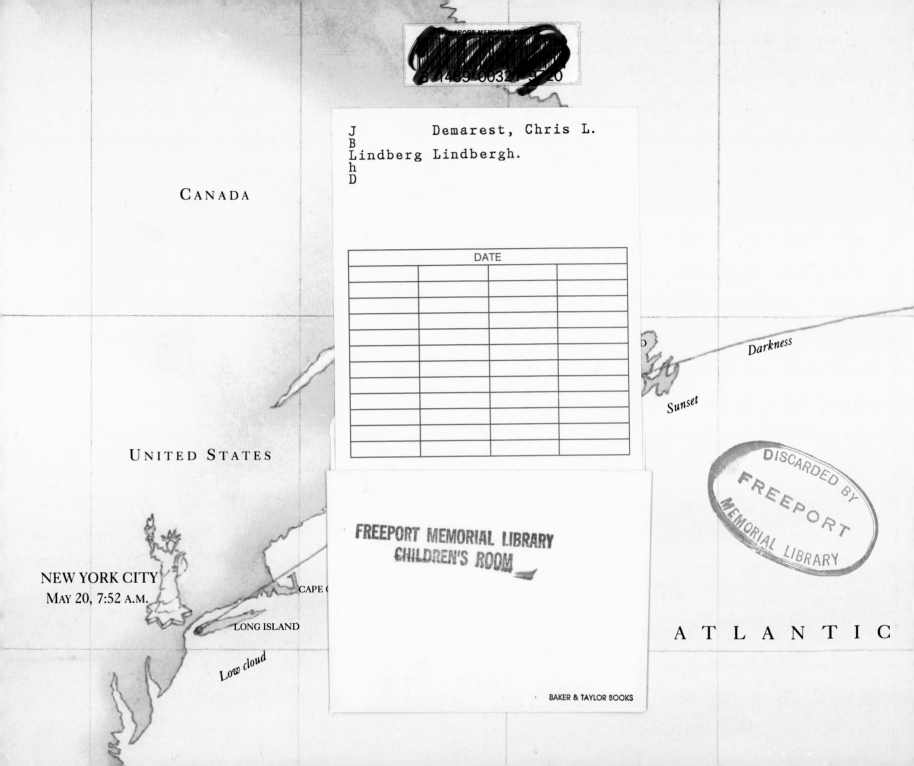

J
B
Lindberg   Demarest, Chris L.
h   Lindbergh.
D

DATE

FREEPORT MEMORIAL LIBRARY
CHILDREN'S ROOM

BAKER & TAYLOR BOOKS

DISCARDED BY
FREEPORT
MEMORIAL LIBRARY